Elementary
Musictheory

FOR BEGINNERS AND ADVANCED STUDENTS

Setting-up, Layout and Cover Page: B & O

Voggenreiter Publishers
Viktoriastr. 25, 53173 Bonn/Germany
www.voggenreiter.de
info@voggenreiter.de

© 2002 Voggenreiter Publishers
International Copyright secured
All Rights Reserved

ISBN: 3-8024-0416-5

Introduction

The traditional notation is the "language" of music. Having a command of this language is of inestimable value for musicians and those interested in music. It brings not only a deeper understanding of musical processes, but also greatly stimulates the development of individual creativity.

This book serves as an introduction to the rudimentary **principles** of the traditional theory of music. It is intended both for those interested in music as well as musicians at the beginning or more advanced stage, but who up to now have given a wide berth to the theoretical side.

For all that, this *Elementary Theory of Music* cannot and is not meant to deal fully and in complete detail with all aspects of this subject. Rather for those interested in music, this book provides a simple introduction to this wide branch of music. If the interest is keen, further studies can be continued as desired to gain a deeper understanding of the theory of music.

After studying this book, the reader should be able to read and understand the essential symbols and musical processes of any piece written in traditional notation.

For quick reference, the *Elementary Theory of Music* contains an appendix summarizing all the subject matter contained in this book. Some subjects, which in the book itself, for the sake of clarity, are given only exemplary mention (for example, the various types of measures and the clefs), are listed in greater detail in the appendix. This method has been chosen to prevent the student from being stressed with superfluous learning material. To gain a better understanding, examples have, however, been added to some chapters.

Particularly important facts are highlighted in grey.

Have fun!

Norbert Opgenoorth / Jeromy Bessler

Contents

1. Notation

Notes

A musical note has several physical properties. The two most important of these are:

- the **pitch**   *how high or how low a note is sung or played* and
- the **duration of the note**   *how long a note sounds.*

Both these can, with the help of notation, be indicated exactly. To present these properties, notation uses special symbols, so-called notes (L. *nota* = sign).

Notes can be compared with the letters of the alphabet. In the case of notation, just as in the written language, a few basic symbols can be put together to form new combinations again and again.

A note is made up of two parts: the **note head** and
the **note stem**.

note stem

note head

For some note values there the so-called *hook* is attached to the stem.

hook

> The various forms of the note head combined with a stem indicate the **duration of the tone**.

So that the notes can be read in the correct order, they are written down on a **notational system - a staff**, they are set down in notes. The staff consists of five horizontal lines and is read from left to right, just like a line of text.

Using the staff, notes can be written on the lines or in the spaces between the lines:

The **stem points** upwards if the note is below the third staff line. If the note is on or above the third staff line, the stem points downwards.

The pitch is determined depending on which line or in which space the head of the note is written:

The note on the top line sounds the highest, that on the bottom line is the lowest tone. In this example, therefore, the second note is higher than the first and the third, but lower than the fourth.

Leger Lines

Leger lines are used for notes which are either too high or too low for the staff.

The leger lines indicate how far above or below the actual staff the notes are.

To avoid using too many leger lines, high notes are often written an octave (see p. 40) lower than they are played.
This is indicated by using the **Ottava** symbol:

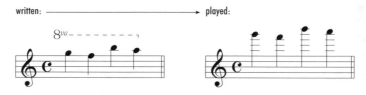

Very low notes are written more easily by using the **Ottava-bassa** symbol:

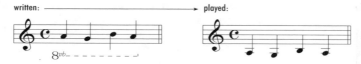

Brace

For certain instruments (e.g. the piano) two or more staves are required at the same time. To indicate that the staves belong together, they are connected by a bracket, the so-called **brace**. In this case, the bar lines are run from top to bottom of the staves:

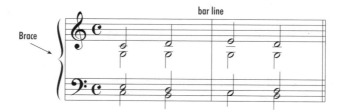

In orchestral works, all the parts are written under each other. Individual groups (e.g. the strings) are joined together with a brace and extended bar lines.
Orchestra music is called a **score**.

Natural Notes

Each note has a name, which is taken from the alphabet. The "musical alphabet" consists, however, of only 7 symbols. Further the order of the letters (compared to the "normal" alphabet) is different:

c d e f g a b

These seven notes are the so-called **natural tones**.
They correspond to the white keys on the piano keyboard.

Clefs

To avoid misunderstandings when writing music, it must be specified on which line the notes are written. This is done by using the **clef**. It is placed at the start of the music. There are various clefs, the two most important ones being the **violin and bass clefs**:

The **violin clef** is often called the **G clef**, as it indicates the position of the note g on the second line (from the bottom) of the staff. The inner spiral of the G clef winds itself round this line.

The second important clef is the **bass clef**:

This clef is called a bass clef, because it is used to indicate the notes of bass instruments of the symphony orchestra.
The bass clef is an **F-clef**. It is always used where the notation of an instrument in the violin clef would require a large number of leger lines. It indicates the position of f - on the second line from the top, between the two dots of the bass clef.

The Appendix contains further information on other important clefs.

The seven natural notes are found in the following order on and between the lines of the staff, with the G-clef indicating the position of G:

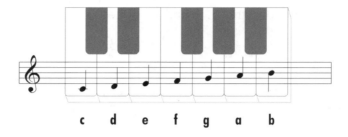

The sequence of natural notes is repeated on the piano keyboard several times. In order to differentiate each individual repeat from the other, the names of the notes in the repeated sequence are marked by a **short line** on the right of the name.

Middle C (so named because of its position on the piano keyboard above the lock) is c'. Accordingly from c' to b' is called a **one-line octave**. In the next repeat, the natural notes belong to the **two-line octave**, etc.:

The octaves below the one-line octave are given the following names:

- **small** octave (indicated with **small** letters: c – b)
- **big** octave (indicated with capital letters: C – B)
- **contra** octave (with lower index number: C_1 - B_1)
- **subcontra** octave (with lower index number: C_2 - B_2)

The Appendix contains further details.

12

Accidentals

Half-step and Whole-step

- The distance from one key of the piano to the next (regardless of whether they are black or white) is described as a **half-step**. A half-step is the smallest interval in traditional Western music. An octave has 12 half-steps: starting from c′ and going up 12 half-steps takes one to c″. (It was only in the 20th century that the system was developed further with smaller units, which have more of a theoretical character and are not so important in practice.)
- A **whole-step** is twice as big as a half-step. On the piano keyboard, a whole-step is an interval of two keys (= two half-steps), e.g. from c′ to d′.

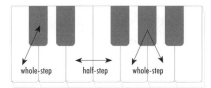

If you count the white and the black keys together, there are 12 notes between c′ and b′. The thirteenth is then c″.

The notes on the white keys are the natural notes.

♯ and ♭

The natural notes correspond to the white keys of the keyboard. They are written on the lines and in the spaces between.

No new letters or notes are used for the tones of the black keys. Instead the natural notes are raised or lowered a half-step by using an accidental.

Raising a note by a half-step

Placing a ♯ (sharp) before a note will raise this tone by a half-step. Thus c' becomes c♯ (spoken: c-sharp), d' becomes d♯ (spoken: d-sharp), etc.

♯

Sharp

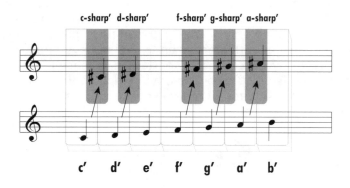

Lowering a tone by a half-step

If there is a ♭ (flat) before a note, this lowers the tone by a half-step. Thus c' becomes c♭ (spoken: c-flat), d' becomes d-flat.

♭

flat

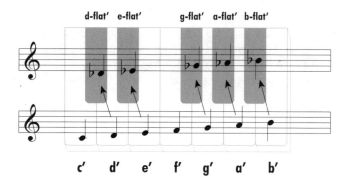

To convey a general idea, the following chart shows a section of the piano keyboard giving the names of the notes. The black keys each have two names, as their name is taken either from the higher or the lower note.

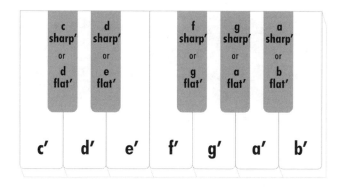

Natural Sign

The accidentals ♯ and ♭ are valid for all the notes of the same pitch within the same measure. Notes which are raised or lowered can be cancelled by using the natural sign. For example, if f is raised to f♯, every following f is automatically f♯ in that measure, unless f is required again, then the ♯ has to be replaced by a ♮. This way f♯ becomes f again.

♮

Natural

Double Accidentals (♭♭ and ×)

Using these three accidentals (♯, ♮, and ♭), the following methods of **altering** a note can be applied:

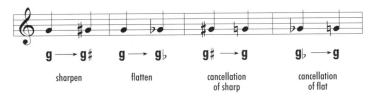

g ⟶ g♯	g ⟶ g♭	g♯ ⟶ g	g♭ ⟶ g
sharpen	flatten	cancellation of sharp	cancellation of flat

To raise or lower a note by two half-steps, the **double sharp** (×) and the **double flat** (♭♭) are used.

g ⟶ g♭♭	g ⟶ g×
double flat	double sharp

By using double sharps and double flats, each key of the piano can be regarded as sharpening or flattening a natural note:

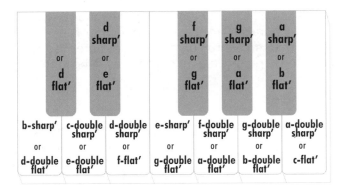

	d sharp′ or e flat′		f sharp′ or g flat′	g sharp′ or a flat′	a sharp′ or b flat′	
b-sharp′ or d-double flat′	c-double sharp′ or e-double flat′	d-double sharp′ or f-flat′	e-sharp′ or g-double flat′	f-double sharp′ or a-double flat′	g-double sharp′ or b-double flat′	a-double sharp′ or c-flat′

Under certain circumstances, the various names of one and the same tone (e.g. F♯ and G♭) are interchangeable. This process is called an **enharmonic change**.

2. Note Values and Meter

Music is a form of art which is performed within the dimension of time. The temporal structure of a piece of music is determined by various factors. The basis is a regular pulse, a steady series of beats.

The note values are placed on these beats as if on a frame. Placing these tones of differing lengths on this frame results in **rhythm**. But, there is still something missing from rhythm – and that is **meter**. The term meter comes from poetry and describes a succession of accented and unaccented syllables. The same procedure is used in music: The beats of the basic frame are combined into a group called a **measure**, (e.g. 4 beats), within the measure they are given various accentuations. A steady meter results through the sequence of measures with similar accentuations. This results in interplay between the meter (often only thought, not actually sounding) with the played notes and rests.

Notes and Rests

Besides the pitch, the duration or length of a note is the second important physical property of a musical tone. In music, the duration of a note has a **relative** and not an **absolute** value. That means the duration of a note is not fixed to a firm time value (e.g. in seconds), but in relation to the duration of the other notes (e.g. "this note is half as long as the previous one"). This means, however, that the exact duration of a note can only be determined, when the tempo of the whole piece is known.

Here again, the notation provides exact information on the duration. The so-called **note value** indicates the duration of a note in relation to the other notes of that piece of music. This occurs through the form of the individual note.

For each note value there is a corresponding rest, for the duration of the **rest** nothing is played or sung.

The diagram shows the most important values of notes and rests:

| whole note | half note | quarter note | eighth note | sixteenth note | thirty-second note | sixty-fourth note |

| whole rest | half rest | quarter rest | eighth rest | sixteenth rest | thirty-second rest | sixty-fourth rest |

In theory, there are even smaller note values, but they are seldom used.

Both in the case of note values and rest values, the next smaller value is formed by dividing the bigger one in two. The chart shows the relationship of the individual notes to each other:

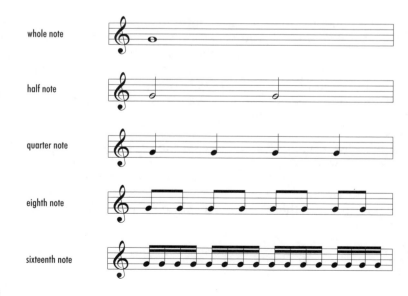

whole note

half note

quarter note

eighth note

sixteenth note

For all note values, smaller than the quarter note, the following applies: Several consecutive notes are easier to read if grouped together under a crossbar. The number of cross bars corresponds to the number of hooks. Notes of differing value can be grouped together:

Note: • Rests are not grouped in this way.
• There is one exception in grouping notes together under a crossbar in vocal music. Here notes are grouped together according to the syllables of the text.

Special Rest Symbols

If an instrument has a long pause in a piece of music over several measures, this is often indicated with special symbols.

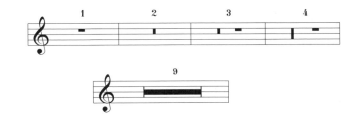

Or:

General Pause: When all instruments and/or voices are silent, this is marked with the sign G.P. To increase the effect of a General Pause, it is often combined with a Fermate (p. 20).

Rests over several measures belong to the **Abreviatures** (abbreviations).

Fermata

If a note is given a fermata (or a "stop sign"), this means that the musician holds the note as long as he thinks appropriate, but definitely longer than is actually indicated.

A fermata is often used at the end of a musical section or at the end of the whole piece.

Dotted Notes and Rest Values

A dot placed after a note adds to it one-half of its value:

A **dotted quarter note** has the same value as a quarter note and an eighth note together.

A **dotted half note** has the same value as a half note and a quarter note together.

The following is one example of how to count a dotted quarter and dotted eighth notes in 4/4 meter:

Similarly a dot placed after a rest adds half of its value to the original value:

A **dotted quarter rest** has the same value as a quarter rest and an eighth rest together.

A **dotted half rest** has the same value as a half rest and a quarter rest together.

The same procedure can be used with all other notes and rest.
Two dots after a note or rest add to it one-half plus one-quarter of its value.

A double dotted quarter note has the following duration:
A quarter + an eighth + a sixteenth

Tie

Two successive notes of the same pitch can be joined by a tie. A tie indicates that the note is held for the duration of both notes added together. The second note is not played, but its value is added to the first note.

There are several reasons for using the tie. The two most important are:

- a note has a value which cannot be indicated with one note. As, for example, there is no 5-quarter note, an eighth note duration is tied to a half note.

- a note is so long that it goes over into the next measure. In this case, too, the second note is not played, but the first note is held over the bar line into the next measure.

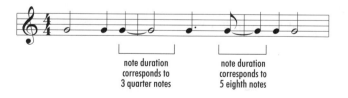

The technical term for extending the note duration by using a **tie** is **ligatura** (L. = tie).

Triplet

Up to now all the note values mentioned could be divided into two: a whole note into two half notes, a half note two quarter notes, etc.

Another important way of grouping note values is to **divide a note by three**.

eighth triplet

Dividing a quarter note by three results in a so-called triplet of three eighth notes, called an **eighth triplet**. A triplet is indicated by a small "3" (usually with a slur under it).

An eighth triplet has the same duration as a quarter note, in 4/4 meter there are therefore 4 eighth triplets.

This principle of performing a group of three notes in place of two of the same kind can be used for all notes.

Thus sixteenth triplets, quarter triplets eighth triplets etc. can be created:

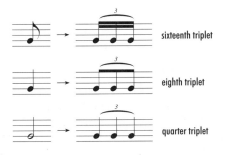

sixteenth triplet

eighth triplet

quarter triplet

Beat/Meter

Beat is the measured sequence of rhythmic strokes or sounds, it is the foundation of music, the continuous basic "beat" of a piece of music. It also means measure, that is grouping several beats together to form a larger unit, regulating the strong and weak beats.

The **meter** is indicated at the beginning of a piece of music, directly behind the clef. In the notation system, measures are marked by a **bar line**, a vertical line drawn through the staff. Larger sections of a piece of music are separated from each other by a **double bar** (two vertical lines); and the end of the piece is indicated by a final **double bar**, but here the second vertical line is thicker.

4/4 Meter

The most important **meter** is **4/4**. For this meter, four beats are combined into one measure, or put in another way: a measure is divided into four quarters. Musicians count these quarter beats, whereby the first beat of a measure is lightly accented: **1** 2 3 4 etc.:

Another symbol for the 4/4 meter from the notation system of the 13th century has survived, which is also frequently used:

The following chart shows some note values in 4/4 meter and suggests ways of counting the units of time:

| 1 | 2 | 3 | 4 | 1 | 2 | 3 and 4 | 1 and 2 and 3 | 4 |

The **time signature** is written directly behind the clef, before the key signature, as a fraction, with the upper number indicating the number of beats in a measure and the lower number the metric fundamental unit (quarter, eighth, etc.).

3/4 Meter

Another frequently used meter is the **3/4 meter**. This meter. seldom used in rock and pop, is very popular in classical music and dance music. The waltz is a well-known example of 3/4 meter. The 3/4 meter has three quarter beats in a measure. The first beat (also referred to as "1") is slightly accented. The 3/4 meter is counted as follows:

1 2 3 **1** 2 3 **1** 2 3

There are no whole notes in 3/4 meter, as one measure has no more than three quarter notes. The longest note value in a 3/4 measure is the dotted half. This fills a full measure.

1 2 3 **1** 2 3 **1** 2 3

25

6/8 Meter

Besides 4/4 and 3/4 meter, **6/8 meter** is one of the most important meters. As in the case of the 3/4 meter, this is also rarely used in pop music, but very frequently in classical music.

In 6/8 meter, the eighth notes are the basic unit in a measure containing six eighth notes. In this case, however, the beats are accented in a different way than in 3/4.

The first and (slightly less) the fourth beats are accented, resulting in two groups of three eighth notes:

1 2 3 4 5 6   **1** 2 3 4 5 6

The longest note value to be found in a 6/8 measure is a dotted half note. Its duration corresponds to 6 eighth notes.

Alla breve Meter

Occasionally the ***alla breve* meter** is used.

Alla breve means, freely translated, "as the half" or "in the manner of a half".

This infers a 2/2 meter, with the accent on the first time unit. As in the case of 4/4 meter, there is also another sign for the alla breve meter which is often used:

Upbeat

Many pieces of music begin with an incomplete measure, that means a measure which contains less notes than indicated by the time signature. This incomplete measure is called an **upbeat**.

The upbeat and the final measure of the piece together add up to a complete measure. A piece with an upbeat contains therefore two incomplete measures: the first and the last.

(1 2 3) 4   1 2 3 4   1 2 3 4   1 2 3 4   1 2 3

Tip: An upbeat is counted like a full measure, which begins with one or several rests.

There are several reasons for using an upbeat, e.g..:

- An upbeat produces tension
- The texts of many songs begin with an unaccented syllable. If one simply started with a full measure (with an accentuated first beat), the text and accentuation would not go together.

Shuffle

In popular music, particularly in blues and jazz, the shuffle style of playing is often used. In this case, the eighth notes are not played evenly, but like a triplet:

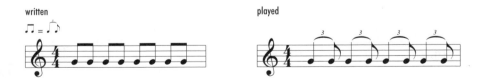

Shuffle is, however, not meter, but more a style of playing, a special way of indicating phrasing. For this reason shuffle is seldom written out, but mostly indicated as a symbol at the beginning of a piece.

System of Meters

Meters are divided up according to their accentuation and/or construction into:

1. Duple Meter
- alternating between accented and unaccented
- examples: 2/8; 2/4; 2/2

2. Triple Meter
- alternating between accented – unaccented – unaccented
- examples: 3/8; 3/4; 3/2

3. Compound Meter
- Two meters put together, either duple or triple
- Main accent on the first beat
- examples: 4/8; 4/4; 4/2; 6/8; 12/8

Combined Meter:
- mixed forms of duple and triple meters
- example: 5/4; 7/4

Quite often compound meter and combined meter are put together in a group.

There are several possibilities of forming combined meters. As the metric signature does not clearly indicate the actual accentuation, the desired breakup is often indicated by the composer over the measure or by grouping the notes (indicating the phrasing). For instance, a 5/4 meter can be understood both as a combination of 2/4 and 3/4 meter or in the reverse order as 3/4 and 2/4 meter.

Some composers indicate the **rhythmic unit value** of the meter in note form, e.g.:

The Most Important Repeat Signs

If a piece is to be played twice in a row, that is without any break, this is indicated at the end of the music with a **repeat sign**.

The repeat sign is nothing more than two dots in front of the final double bar.

The repeat sign can also be used in the middle of a piece. In this case, all the measures up to this sign are played again:

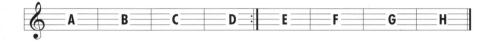

Sequence of the measures: **A B C D A B C D E F G H**

Quite often only a few measures are to be repeated. In this case, an inverted repeat sign marks the beginning of the section to be repeated:

Sequence of measures: **A B C D E F C D E F G H**

Sequence of measures: **A B C D A B C D E F E F G H**

In some cases, the last or last few measures are different from the original. To indicate this, signs (like a box) are placed over the measures: box No. 1 applies to the first passage. When this is repeated, box No. 1 is not played, but instead box No. 2:

Sequence of measures: **A B C D A B E F G H**

In classical music there are other repeat signs.
The most important are:

da Capo   (= from the head, from the beginning) Instead of the simple repeat sign, the instruction *da capo* (or in short *D.C.*) is written under the last measure, and everything is repeated from the start.

dal Segno   (= from the sign) If the instruction *dal segno* (or: *D.S.*) is written under the last measure, the repeat starts from the sign (𝄋).

Sequence of measures: **A B C D E F G H C D E F G H**

da capo al fine   The repeat starts at the beginning and ends with the measure, under which the word *fine* (end, final) is written. *Fine* can also be written under a single note (even in the middle of a measure), which then becomes the final tone.

Sequence of measures: **A B C D E F G H A B C D**

The following sign is a special form used in all cases where one or more measures are to be repeated:

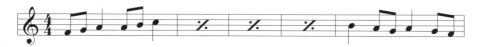

This sign means: The first measures are to be repeated three time

This sign means: The first two measures are to be repeated once.

When single notes or groups of notes must be repeated, there are still other shorthand devices. These are also called **abbreviatures**. The graphics show the most important of them:

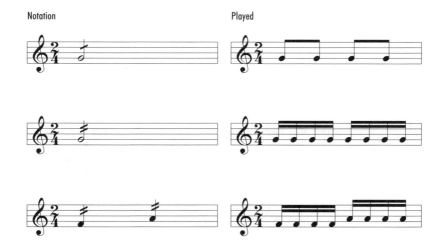

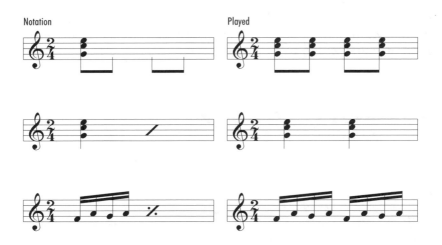

Notation   Played

If only the **articulation** of a measure is to be repeated in the next measure or following measures, this is indicated with the word simile (It. = similar):

sim.

3. Expression Marks

Dynamics

Dynamics (Greek = force) are words, abbreviations and signs that indicate the degree of volume in a piece of music. These can refer to either one single note or a larger section. These symbols are usually printed just below the music staff. The most common are:

ff	*fortissimo*	very loud
f	*forte*	loud
p	*piano*	soft
pp	*pianissimo*	very soft

Often the dynamic symbols are more differentiated:

meno f	*meno forte*	less loud
più p	*più piano*	softer
meno p	*meno piano*	less soft

There are also volume symbols for individual notes, e.g.:

sf , *sfz* , *fz*	*sforzato*	forced

Another part of these dynamic symbols deals with **change of volume**. These symbols indicate a gradual change from loud to soft and vice versa. The most common of these are crescendo and decrescendo, indicated by the following symbols:

cresc.	or	<	= louder
decresc.	or	>	= softer

Articulation

This is a term used to indicate various ways of binding or separating individual notes. In principle this articulation can be divided into legato (It. = bound together) and non legato (It. = not bound together).

legato

Legato notes are played without any break or interruption between them. Notes to be played legato are indicated by a slur.

Normally the articulation is legato. If not indicated otherwise by the composer, legato is played.

The legato slur must not be mistaken for a tie!
The tie connects two notes of the **same** pitch, so that they become one longer note. The legato slur connects two or several notes of **different** pitch with each other.

non legato

In the case of non legato, consecutive notes are separated from each other. This separation is defined more precisely by the Italian terms of *portato* (sustained), *tenuto* (held), *staccato* (separated) or *staccatissimo* (more distinctly separated).
There are also special symbols to denote the various forms of non legato:

All details on articulation are indicated above the note head (except in the case of music written for several parts).

Phrasing

The **slur** is another important musical symbol. It looks very similar to the symbol for a tie, but must not be mistaken for it.

The slur gives the musician valuable information on the desired phrasing. Just as in writing, the capital letter denotes the beginning and the fullstop the end of a sentence, so the slur indicates the beginning and end of a musical "phrase". Very often the construction of musical phrases and sections are indicated through rests, harmonics or the run of a melody, so that slurs are not always used.

Note: Not everything written under a slur has to be played legato.

Tempo

The written value of the note indicates nothing about the actual duration of the note.

This is determined only in conjunction with a fixed tempo. Tempo indications are noted at the beginning of a piece above the first stave. They are effective throughout the piece or until a tempo change is indicated by the composer. Traditionally the tempo of a piece of music is given in the Italian language.

The most common Italian tempo indications (which also partially dictate the character of the music) are:

presto	very fast	168-208 bpm
vivace	lively	
allegro	fast, playful	120-168 bpm
allegretto	not so fast, merrily	
moderato	moderately	108-120 bpm
andantino	moving moderately	
andante	moving more moderately	76-108 bpm
grave	grave, solemn	
adagio	slowly	66- 76 bpm
lento	slowly	
larghetto	fairly slow	60 – 66 bpm
largo	very slow	40 – 60 bpm

Normally all tempo indications are measured against *andante*, a walking speed (or pulse). That is about 80 beats per minute. All other tempi are based on this. Considerable differences, however, occur, depending on the interpretation.

assai	-	very
comodo	-	leisurely
con brio	-	with fire
con moto	-	with movement
ma non troppo	-	but not too much
meno	-	less
molto	-	much, very
più	-	more
poco a poco	-	gradually
sostenuto	-	sustained
subito	-	suddenly
un poco	-	a little

Metronome

Should a composer desire his composition to be performed in a specific tempo, he states the **metronome speed**. The metronome, patented in 1816 by Johann Nepomuk Maelzel, is a mechanical device which makes a ticking sound at the speed for which it is set. Metronome speed is indicated as ♩ = 80 or M.M. 80 (Maelzels Metronome). In popular music, the unit of bpm (beats per minute) is used. 80 bpm means the same as ♩ = 80.

Change of Tempo

In principle, there are two ways of changing the tempo of a piece of music, gradually and abruptly.

1. **Gradual change of tempo:** The traditional terms for a gradual change of tempo are *accelerando* and *ritardando*

   Ritardando (abbr: *rit.*) means: slow down. The tempo slows down gradually. Instructions having a similar meaning are: *ritenuto* (*rit.*), *rallentando* (*rall.*), *meno mosso, allargando, calando* and *morendo*.

   Accelerando (*acc.*) means becoming faster: The tempo is increased (slowly and) evenly. Similar instructions are *stringendo* (*string.*), *stretto* and *più mosso*.

If, after an *accelerando* or a *ritardando*, a return to the original tempo is desired, the corresponding instruction of a tempo, *tempo primo* (first tempo) or something similar is used. These instructions are to be regarded as a general guide, the exact interpretation is, of course, in the hands of the musician.

2. **Abrupt Change of Tempo**. Here the tempo changes from one moment to the next. In most cases, sudden tempo changes are indicated to achieve a dramatic effect - particularly suited to the music. In popular music, sudden tempo changes are often simply denoted by a new BPM instruction.

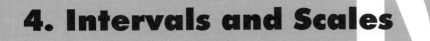

4. Intervals and Scales IV

Intervals

An **interval** (L. = intervallum = space between) is the **distance in pitch between two tones**. This distance is measured in half-steps. The number of half-steps is identical with the number of piano keys. The intervals are formed from the natural notes (counting from c', which is also known as Middle C:

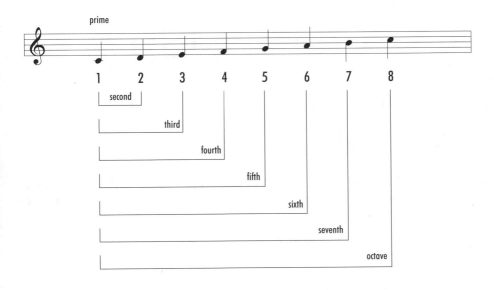

Intervals are named by numbering consecutively in Latin the notes from the natural notes:

c' to c'	**prime**	(Latin: *primus* = first)
c' to d'	**second**	(Latin: *secundus* = second)
c' to e'	**third**	(Latin: *tertius* = third)
c' to f'	**fourth**	(Latin: *quartus* = fourth)
c' to g'	**fifth**	(Latin: *quintus* = fifth)
c' to a'	**sixth**	(Latin: *sexte* = sixth)
c' to b'	**seventh**	(Latin: *septimus* – seventh)
c' to c''	**octave**	(Latin: *oktavus* – eighth)

The prime is given the ordinal number of 1. If two tones have the distance of a prime, then they have the same pitch.
With the eighth interval, the octave, the next natural of the same name is reached and the series is repeated.
Intervals larger than an octave, are made up of an octave and one of the basic intervals, e.g.

c' to d''	**ninth**	= octave + second
c' to e''	**tenth**	= octave + third

1. Intervals with one basic form

Intervals are divided into two groups: intervals with **one** basic form and intervals with **two** basic forms.

Intervals with one basic form are the **prime, fourth, fifth** and **octave**. As they have only one basic form, they are also described as **perfect intervals**.

perfect prime	perfect fourth	perfect fifth	perfect octave
(= 0 half-steps)	(= 5 half-steps)	(= 7 half-steps)	(= 12 half-steps)

2. Intervals with two basic forms

Intervals with two basic forms are the **second**, **third**, **sixth** and **seventh**. These intervals can be minor or major intervals, e.g as a minor sixth or major sixth.

Here the minor and major second (each time from c') are shown.
Counting from the first tone (here: c) up the natural scale, the second tone is d.
The resulting interval is a second.

Depending on whether it has one or two half-steps, it is called a **minor** or a **major** second.

The same applies to the third: A third is **always** the **third** note. (The first note counts as the first tone.) Depending on whether it has three or four half-steps, it is a **minor** or a **major** third.

The sixth is **always** the **sixth** note. Depending on whether it has 8 or 9 half-steps, it is called a **minor** or a **major** sixth.

The seventh is **always** the **seventh** note.
The minor seventh has 10 half-steps, the major seventh 11 half-steps.

3. Diminished and Augmented Intervals

The three basic interval forms are: major, minor or perfect. These basic forms can be made either smaller or larger. This results in **diminished** or **augmented** intervals.

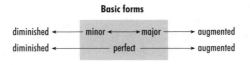

The following example illustrates this clearly: a **perfect** fifth (c-g; 7 half-steps) becomes when diminished, a **diminished** fifth (c-g♭; 6 half-steps) or when augmented, an **augmented** fifth (c-g♯; 8 half-steps):

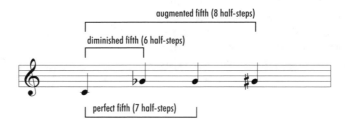

Major and **minor** intervals can also be changed in this way:

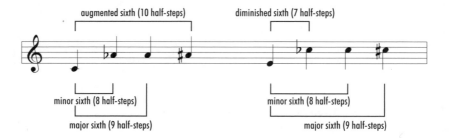

Compared with other intervals, diminished and augmented intervals are not so common.

Tritone

The **tritone** (L./Gr. *tritonus* = three tone step) has a special position amongst the intervals. It divides the octave into two equal intervals, that it consists of three whole-steps. Strictly speaking, only the **augmented fourth** is a tritone (as it comprises only three whole-steps); in practice, however the **diminished fifth** is often referred to as a tritone , too.

As it is very difficult to sing the tritone, it was often referred to in medieval music as *diabolus in musica* (devil in the music).

Complementary Intervals

Two intervals which complement each other to form an octave (e.g. minor third and major sixth or major second and minor seventh) are called complementary intervals.

Formation of Intervals

An interval can be created from any chosen starting position in the following way:

- First count the number of natural notes corresponding to the name of the interval and then
- The resulting interval is amended if necessary.

For example, to form a minor sixth from g' upwards:

1. Starting from g, count up six notes (= Sixth):

2. As there are 9 half-steps between g and e, the resulting interval is a major sixth. So it has to be reduced by one half-step to form the desired minor sixth:

minor sixth
(= 8 half-steps)

When forming intervals, always count the number of natural notes to the desired interval.

Forming Lower Intervals

Intervals can be formed upwards and downwards. To create a lower interval, always count the number of natural notes down instead of up.
In this case, too, the starting note is also the first tone:

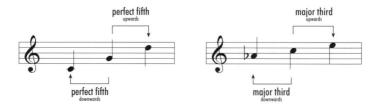

Scales

A scale (It. scala) is the collection of tonal material which is applied in a piece of music. This notes are arranged according to pitch and within the scales have differing significance.

This material is the basis for a piece of music and can be extended by additional notes.

Major Scales

> The sequence of natural tones from c' to c" forms the **major scale**. This scale begins and ends with c, and is called the **tonic** of the scale. The tonic gives its name to the scale – in this case: **C Major**. The major scale is the fundament of Western harmony, on which all other scales are based.

For a better understanding of the following and as a help in analyzing scales, knowledge of how **interval symbols are written** will be useful. This system is widely used. The notes the major scale are numbered from 1 to 8.

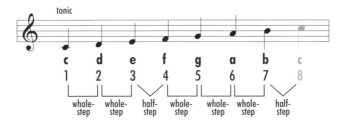

The numbers represent the intervals of the major scale. The structure of intervals of other scales is always compared with the major scale. Variations are indicated with ♯ and ♭ before the respective interval symbol.

Example: The symbol "3" always denotes a major third, a minor third is indicated with the symbol "♭3".

This interval structure is the "construction plan" of all major scales, it dictates the type of intervals and their sequence within the scale. Based on this, a major scale can be constructed on any of the twelve chromatic tones simply by changing the beginning tone and adhering to the "construction plan" and sequence of intervals.

The example of the D major scale below demonstrates this principle. For this the construction plan of a major scale

is applied to the tonic of d, creating a D Major scale. Two notes have to be raised (f to f♯ and c to c♯) in order to keep to the construction plan:

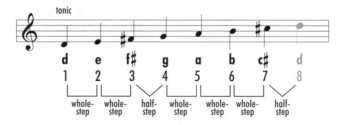

Leading tone

The seventh note of the major scale is also called the leading note, as it leads back to the tonic: If the scale is played upwards, the seventh step develops a strong tendency to "lead up" to the tonic and which is resolved on reaching the tonic (= 8th step).

Two more examples:

When forming other major scales, individual natural notes have to be raised or lowered in order to retain the pattern of intervals of the major scale.

Scale of G Major:

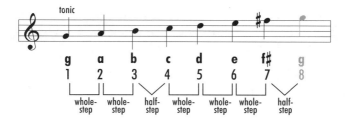

For the scale of G major, the natural note of F has to be raised to F sharp (F♯) in order to create a major scale.

B♭ Major:

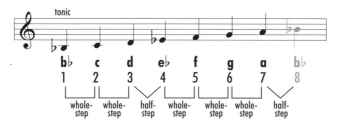

For the B♭ (B Flat) scale, apart from the tonic, the E is lowered to E♭. Even if the tonic is already raised or lowered, nothing changes in the scale pattern: The pattern of intervals must conform with the major scale "construction plan", which means altering individual notes, if necessary.

No matter what tonic is used to construct a major scale, the interval structure stays the same, which involves changing some notes (as opposed to C major).
This **interval structure** is the special characteristic of the major scale.

Scales and Key Signatures

A **scale** provides information on the progression of the notes and their relation to each other. It can be regarded as a collection of material which can be used by a composer.

> The **key** determines the key signature, the tonic and the harmonic relationships in a piece of music. The name of a key is taken from its tonic. For example, one can say that a piece of music "is in E major".

The **key** of a piece can be recognised by the key signature. This appears at the beginning of each staff, directly after the clef. The key signature indicates which natural notes have to be changed when playing the piece. This applies to the entire piece, but can be lifted by a cancel sign.:

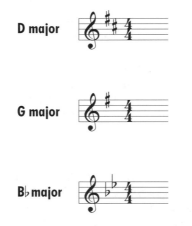

D major

G major

B♭ major

Natural Minor Scale

There are many other scales, in addition to major scales. The most important is the natural minor scale. The most simple minor scale is A minor. It consists of the natural notes, but starts on A and not C:

The natural minor scale differs from the major scale through its interval structure, the pattern for the distance between the tones.

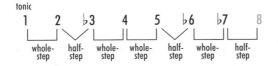

Starting from the note of a, this results in the **scale of A minor**:

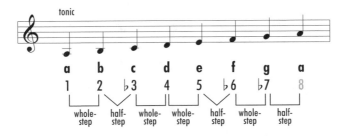

In order to compare the interval patterns of natural minor and major scales, this graphic shows the **scale of A major**:

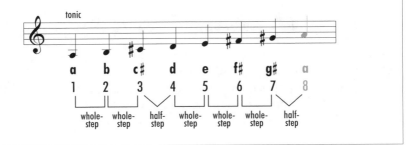

Starting from the tone of c results in the scale of **C minor**:

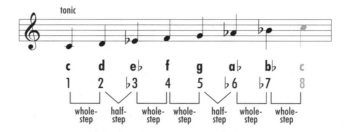

Relative Keys

For every major key there is a related minor key. Both use the same notes, so therefore they have the **same key signature**. The two scales (graphically) run parallel to each other:

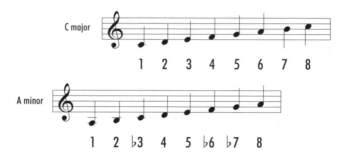

These two keys are called relative keys.

The **relative minor key** to any desired major key is determined in the following way:
The tonic is a minor third lower than the tonic of the major scale.
For C major the relative key is therefore A minor.
When ascertaining the key of a piece by its key signature **either** it is in the corresponding major key **or** the relative minor key.

Harmonic Minor Scale

For harmonic reasons, the 7th step of the minor scale is often raised. This scale is then described as harmonic minor scale.

Melodic Minor Scale

When creating harmonic minor, an augmented second interval is formed between the 6th and 7th notes by raising the 7th note of the natural minor.
To obtain a strictly diatonic scale (i.e. made up only of minor and major seconds), the sixth step of the harmonic minor scale is likewise raised by a half-step to form the melodic minor scale.

A special characteristic of the melodic minor scale is the fact that the scale is played in general only ascending with a raised 6th and 7th step, but descending the natural minor scale is used:

Gypsy Minor Scale

Another important member of the family of minor scales is the so-called **Gypsy minor**. It is obtained by raising the 4th note of the scale of the hamonic minor:

Through the two augmented seconds and four half-steps in this scale, it has the "most oriental character" of the minor family.

Blue Notes and Blues Scale

Originally the so-called blue notes represented an attempt to present the characteristic intervals of Afro-American folkmusic within our notation system. These names were given to the notes as they were used in (sung) blues of the slaves in America at the beginning of the last century. This intonation, which cannot be produced by our tempered tuning (i.e not on the piano) is as follows:

- The first blue note, which lies between the major and minor third (and replaces both),
- The second blue note, which is somewhat lower than the perfect fifth,
- The third blue note, which corresponds roughy to our minor seventh.

By incorporating the blue notes, various scales have been developed, which are described as blues scales, e.g.:

Modes of the Major Scales (Ecclesiastical Modes)

When forming major scales with various tonics, the following principle was applied:

The notes alter, the interval pattern stays the same.

This principle can be applied the other way round:

The notes remain the same, the interval pattern changes.

Here the scale of C major is started at C, then D and then E etc., without altering any of the notes belonging to the scale. This results in 7 scales, all of which contain the notes of C major, but in which each one produces different interval patterns.

These seven scales are the so-called **modes** of C major (sometimes also call Ecclesiastical or Church modes).

The modes go back much further than the present major/minor system. Here they are labelled with their names and all written with c' as the tonic to facilitate an easier comparison of the interval patterns:

Just as all major scales can be derived from C major, the interval pattern of each mode can be formed from any note. The process is identical: The construction plan is carried out starting from any desired note, the interval pattern remains the same, whereas the notes change.

The following example of the Dorian mode with the tonic of d and the Dorian mode with the tonic of e (also known as D-Dorian and E-Dorian) illustrates this clearly:

The modes are often subdivided into major and minor related scales according to their interval pattern.

Those modes with a major third between the tonic and the third note belong to the **major-related modes**:

- Ionian (major)
- Lydian
- Mixolydian.

Those modes with a minor third belong to the **minor-related modes**:

- Dorian
- Phrygian
- Aeolian (natural minor).

The Locrian mode is an exception, it belongs to neither the major or the minor-related modes.

Other Scales

1. Pentatonic Scale

The Pentatonic scale consists of five notes (Gr. Penta = five) and has no half-steps. It is one of the oldest known scales, which is still used today in the traditional music of many cultures.

As there are no half-steps in the Pentatonic scale, the typical leading-up tendency of Western melodic patterns and harmony is missing; it is not easy to assign it from a functional point of view like other scales. The special fascination resulting from this simple structure is one of the reasons for the great popularity of this scale in all forms of improvised music.

There are two important basic forms of the Pentatonic scale: the **major Pentatonic** and the **minor Pentatonic**.

- The major Pentatonic results from the layering of 4 fifths: c-g-d-a-e. Written down, in order of pitch within an octave produces the following scale:

Major Pentatonic

Through the major third (between the tonic and the third note), this scale belongs to the major-related scales.

- The minor Pentatonic can be interpreted as the 5th mode of the major Pentatonic. It contains a minor third and a minor seventh and is thus a minor-related scale.

Minor Pentatonic

These are only the two most commonly known of a large number of five-tone scales which are theoretically possible.

2. Chromatic Scale

The chromatic (Gr. *chroma* = color) scale contains all twelve tones of our notation system. Thus there is only one chromatic scale, from which any chosen chord or scale can be derived.

3. Whole-step Scale

The whole-step scale divides the octave into whole-steps. Through the unchanging interval pattern without half-steps, each of the six notes of this scale can be interpreted as the tonic. Thus the whole-step scale of D uses the same notes as those of C or E etc. Therefore only two different whole-step scales exist.

4. Whole-step/Half-step Scale (WS/HS)

This eight-tone scale is made up of whole-steps and half-steps. Due to the **symmetrical** interval pattern the notes of the scale are repeated in intervals of a minor third, i.e. the E♭ WS/HS scale uses the same notes as the C WS/HS scale. Therefore only three different whole-step/half-step scales exist.

5. Half-step/Whole-step Scale (HS/WS)

This scale consists, just like the whole-step/half-step scale, of eight notes. In this scale, too, the notes of the scale are repeated in intervals of a minor third. Therefore only three different half-step/whole-step scales actually exist.
The half-step/whole-step scale has both minor and major thirds. Through the many half- steps, this scale is suited to a majority of the most important chord structures.

Circle of Fifths

The **circle of fifths** presents in graphic form the relationships of the various keys and is of inestimable value for musical analysis and composition.

Starting on any one note (here, for example, C) and going forwards or backwards in fifths, the circle closes after 6 fifths, as G♭ through enharmonic change is the same note as F♯. The further apart two harmonies are from each other in the series of fifths, the less they are related to each other.

The relationships between keys which are neighbors on the circle of fifths is of central significance, for example, C major, F major and G major.

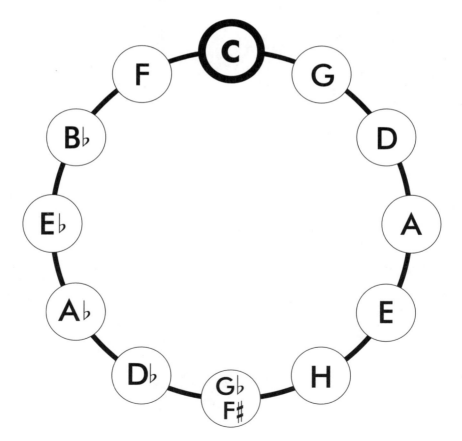

Besides the fifth, some other intervals can be used to form a circle. The other most important circles are the minor third circle and the major third circle.

For the purposes of analysis, several circles are sometimes combined with each other in order to illustrate all the important relationships of a central note. The following chart is an example of such a combination:

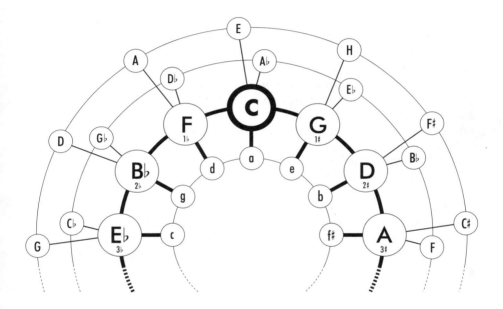

Here the various third relationships are shown together with the fifth relationships.

Just and tempered tuning

The intervals of European music are calculated on physical fundamentals:

- If a string is half as long as another (in the ratio 1:2), then its pitch is twice as high. This corresponds to the interval of an octave.

- Two strings in the ratio of 2:3 have an interval of a fifth from each other.

Other intervals can be calculated in the same way.

This system, so simple it sounds, has however some faults, as the physical size of the various intervals does not tally exactly. It could be said that the intervals do not exactly match (or: are not exactly the same size).
For example, the interval of four major thirds (c-d-g♯-b♯/c) is slightly smaller than an octave (c-c).
If 12 fifths were stacked on top of each other, this should correspond to a span of 7 octaves, it is, however, somewhat smaller.

For this reason, the **tempered tuning,** which dates back to Andreas Werckmeister has been used since the end of the 17th century. In tempered tuning the octave is divided into twelve equal parts, introducing the **cent** as unit of measurement. Just tuning however ist hardly used, especially since not all instruments can be played in just tuning.

5. Chords

Chord and Triad

In traditional harmony, the term **chord** means the simultaneous playing of three or more notes. The most normal and commonly used chord is the **triad**. It consists of three notes played at the same time. A triad does not consist of just any three notes, there are certain rules for its structure:

1. Each triad has a root, from which it take its name.
2. The triad is formed by taking two thirds above the root.
3. Only notes from the scale of the same name are used (for the present).

Major Triad

Example: The formation of the **C major triad**.

1. For a C major triad the root is c.
2. In the C major scale, a third up from c is the tone of e.
3. From e, a further third up is g.

Superimposed upon each other the two thirds form the C major triad.

A major triad consists of a **major** and a **minor** third. Usually the major triad is given a symbol, using the capital letter of its root (e.g. C).

As the notes of a triad are played together, they are written on top of each other and have a common stem.

C major triad

The notes of a chord are often given interval names. The middle tone of this major triad is "the third", the highest is "the fifth".

Minor Triad

To form a **minor triad**, the same rules apply as for the major triad (see p. 61). However, instead of the major scale, the minor scale is used.

In the A minor scale, two thirds up from the root of A form the A minor triad. As the minor scale has a different structure than the major scale, the intervals of a minor triad are therefore different to those of the major triad:

A minor triad consists of a **minor** and a **major** third. Mostly the minor triad is given a symbol, using the capital letter of its tonic, followed by a small "m" (e.g. Am). A small letter is often also used as a symbol for the minor triad.

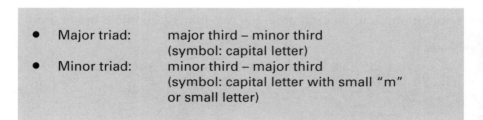

- Major triad: major third – minor third
  (symbol: capital letter)
- Minor triad: minor third – major third
  (symbol: capital letter with small "m"
  or small letter)

Diminished and Augmented chords

Two more basic triads can be formed from the combination of a major and a minor third: the diminished and the augmented chord.

- The **diminished chord** (symbol "o")
  This chord consists of two minor thirds.

- The **augmented chord** (symbol "+")
  This chord consists of two major thirds.

In practice, the diminished chord is nearly always turned into a tetrad (four-note chord), the diminished seventh (symbol "o7") by adding another minor third.

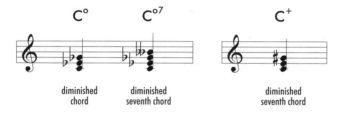

diminished chord   diminished seventh chord   diminished seventh chord

Tetrads

If a further note is added to a triad, this makes it a **tetrad** (four-note chord).

There are various ways of turning a triad into a tetrad. The easiest way is to add a further third to a triad. This results in two more important sounds: the seventh chord.

Seventh Chord

Adding another third to the basic triad creates two of the most important tetrad:

- the dominant seventh chord (maj. third, min. third, min. third, symbol: 7)
- the major seventh chord (maj. third, min. third, maj. third, symbol: maj7).

They are given names based on the interval between the lowest and the highest note.

dominant seventh chord   major seventh chord

In the traditional harmony, dominant seventh chords create a certain tension, which has to be resolved.

Dissonant Chords

Each triad can be extended by adding further thirds. In the chord symbol system, added notes are named after the interval they form to the root of the triad.

Starting from the most simple chord, the major triad, these additions can theoretically be continued up to the $^{7/9/11/13}$ chord.

The $^{7/9/11/13}$ chord can be interpreted as a complete scale, played simultaneously. The interval number of "15" corresponds then again to the tonic.

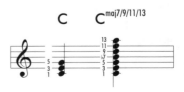

All added notes which are not part of the basic triad are called **tension notes** or **option notes**.

Often tension notes are not listed in the chord symbol. Very often in jazz only the biggest interval is named, with the notes in between being automatically added: A C^{13} chord is then played as $C^{7/9/11/13}$.

Other Chords

In addition to extending chords by thirds or doubling individual chord notes, notes can be added to a chord (e.g. the sixth), or chord notes can be replaced (e.g. the third by the fourth). Particularly in the case of consonant chords, chord notes can be altered, that is lowered or raised.

Here are three of the most important chords:

- ## Chords with added Ninth

The dominant seventh chord is extended by a third over the seventh. That means the 9th note of the scale is added.

There are various ways of creating a ninth chord: by way of a major chord, or a minor chord, as well as with a minor or major ninth.

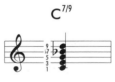

- ## Chords with added Sixth

The sixth step of the scale is added to the major triad. The technical term for this extension is *sixte ajoutée* (added sixth).

• The sus4 chord

In this chord the third (of the major scale) is replaced by the 4th step, thus forming a so-called suspended chord (sus = suspension).
The fourth creates tension in this chord, which has a strong tendency to be resolved into the third of the major triad.

Inversions

A chord can be played in various ways, depending on the order of the notes. There are three variants for a triad:

- In the first variant the tonic is the lowest note. This is the **root position** of the chord.
- Transposing the tonic of the chord up an octave results in the **first inversion**. In this inversion the root tone is the highest note, the third the lowest. The first inversion of a triad is also referred to as a **sixth chord**.
- The **second inversion** is formed by transposing the lowest note of the first inversion (the third) up an octave. Now the fifth is the lowest note. The second inversion of a triad is also called a **six-four chord**.

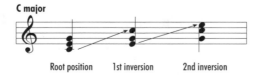

C major

Root position   1st inversion   2nd inversion

> The chord always stays the same, no matter in which sequence
> the notes are superimposed. In this case all chords are C major
> triads, the root is c.

Inversions of Tetrads

Inversions can also be formed from these chords. In the case of
tetrads, there are **three inversions**, besides the root position.
In the traditional harmonic analysis, only inversions of the dominant
seventh chords have their own name. These inversions are named
after the intervals within the chord:

- 1stinversion: **five-six chord**
- 2nd inversion: **three-four chord**
- 3rd inversion: **second chord**

Root position   1st inversion   2nd inversion   3rd inversion

Chord Positions and Voicings

When the notes of a chord are so ordered that there would be room for another chord tone, this is referred to as a chord in wide position: In this example, it would be possible to add further chord tone (e' and c'') between the notes already there.

weite Lage

In traditional harmony, the term **position** is also used with a different meaning. Depending on which is the highest note of the chord, one speaks of the **Octave position** (highest note is the root), the **third position** (highest note is the third) or the **fifth position** (highest note is the fifth).

In (Jazz) harmony, the different ways of arranging chord tones are called **voicings**. There are numerous ways of presenting a voicing of a given chord; here a selection:

- **drop 2**: The drop 2 technique is a way of "stretching" chords. For this, the second note of the chord is dropped an octave.

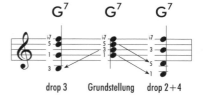

Grundstellung   drop 2

- **drop 3** and **drop 2+4**: This and similar drop variations are not so common, but function on the same principle: the notes in question are moved down to the bass.

drop 3   Grundstellung   drop 2+4

The "drop technique" can also be applied in the reverse way: Individual notes are moved into the upper parts.

Diatonic Chords

All chords which are formed from the notes of a scale are referred to as **diatonic chords** of this scale. The most important of these chords are the so-called graduated triads. They are formed by creating a diatonic triad on each note of a scale. In C major, for example:

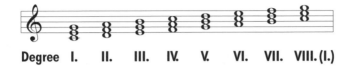

Degree I. II. III. IV. V. VI. VII. VIII.(I.)

The degree names are also used in the short form for commonly used chord sequences and cadences.
In C major II-VI-V-I is the shortened form for the chord sequence:

$$Dm^{(7)} - Am^{(7)} - G^{(7)} - C^{(maj7)}$$

(The numbers in the brackets apply to the diatonic tetrads.)

In traditional harmony, each of these chords has a certain function, they are therefore also called **functions** of the key.
The most important functions are:

- the triad on the 1st step (the **tonic**, symbol: T),
- the triad on the 4th step (the **subdominant**, symbol: S) and
- the triad on the 5th step (the **dominant**, symbol: D).

These three major chords are on the tonal degrees, the other four chords on the modal degrees.

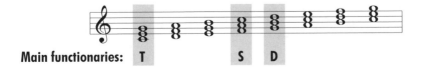

Main functionaries: T   S D

Cadence

The most common form of connecting a chord is the **cadence** (L. *cade-re* = to fall). In the most simple version the cadence is made up of the three main functionaries of a key, which are played in a certain sequence (1st degree - 4th degree - 5th degree - 1st degree).

In the following cadence example in C major, the graduated triads are turned into tetrads by doubling the root tone, this is a so-called **four-part harmony**.

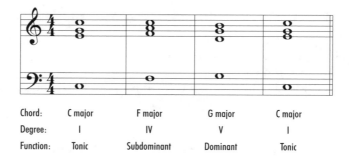

Chord:	C major	F major	G major	C major
Degree:	I	IV	V	I
Function:	Tonic	Subdominant	Dominant	Tonic

When the three main functionaries of a key are played directly one after the other, all the notes of the key in question are played. For this reason the cadence is an important way of clearly determining a key. In traditional harmony, the cadence is the fundamental and therefore most important process.

Chord Symbols

The chord symbol system represents a shorthand form of writing chords. The symbols are used as the basis for accompanying a melody or for improvisation. Using chord symbols, all relevant information can be shown on the structure of a chord in a clear and precise way.
A combination of letters, abbreviations and numbers are used to describe chords.
The following rules for these contractions apply:

- The basic triad is named after the letter of its root, the way it is written states whether the key is major or minor. All other notes and changes are indicated by the numbers of the intervals of the major scale.

- Changes to the notes of the chord are specified by ♭ and ♯.

- The seven (7) is always at the beginning of numerical orders, as it is a fixed part of the chord and not an optional note. (as, e.g. 9, 11, 13).

- If, in addition to a seven, a chord has a six (6), it is called a 13,

- The add-extensions are added to the basic triad, whereas the sus-extensions replace the third of the basic triad.

The seventh has a special place within these rules:
The symbol "7" always indicates the minor seventh. If a major seventh is to be added to the chord, this must be indicated by using "maj7".
There are various forms of chord symbols, differing in details, but which all share the same basic principle.

List of Chord Symbols

Symbol	Chord Structure
Major	1–3–5
6	1–3–5–6
add9	1–3–5–9
6 / 9	1–3–5–6–9
sus4	1–4–5
maj7	1–3–5–maj7
maj7 / #5	1–3–#5–maj7
maj7 / 9	1–3–5–maj7–9
maj7 / #11	1–3–maj7–#11
maj7 / 13	1–3–5–maj7–13
maj7 / 9 / 13	1–3–5–maj7–9–13
minor	1–♭3–5
minor 6	1–♭3–5–6
minor 6 / 9	1–♭3–5–6–9
minor 7	1–♭3–5–♭7
minor 7 / ♭5	1–♭3–♭5–♭7
minor 7 / 9	1–♭3–5–♭7–9
minor maj7	1–♭3–5–maj7
minor maj7 / 9	1–♭3–5–maj7–9
minor add9	1–♭3–5–9
minor 7 / 11	1–♭3–5–♭7–11

Symbol	Chord Structure
minor 7/9/11	1–♭3–5–♭7–9–11
minor add11	1–♭3–5–11
7	1–3–5–♭7
7 sus4	1–4–5–♭7
7 / 9	1–3–5–♭7–9
7 / 9 / 13	1–3–5–♭7–9–13
7 / 9 / #11	1–3–♭7–9–#11
7 / 9 / ♭13	1–3–♭7–9–♭13
7 / ♭9	1–3–5–♭7–♭9
7 / ♭9 / #11	1–3–♭7–♭9–#11
7 / ♭9 / 13	1–3–5–♭7–♭9–13
7 / ♭9 / ♭13	1–3–5–♭7–♭9–♭13
7 / #9	1–3–5–♭7–#9
7 / #9 / #11	1–3–♭7–#9–#11
7 / #9 / ♭13	1–3–5–♭7–#9–♭13
7 / #11	1–3–♭7–#11
7 / 13	1–3–5–♭7–13
7 / 13 / sus4	1–4–5–♭7–13
7 / ♭13	1–3–5–♭7–♭13
o7	1–♭3–♭5–♭7
+	1–3–#5

Chord Synonyms

The dictionary defines synonym (Gr. „of similar name") as: two or more different sounding words having a similar meaning, e.g. „carpenter" and „joiner".

In this context, it means: the same chord can have different names, depending on which aspect it is being looked at. This means taking into consideration the harmonious surroundings of the chord, its function within a piece or what the musician determines.

Here is an example of this:

The chord of C-E-G-A would, in this form, be given the symbol C^6 (C major chord with added major sixth).

If the notes of this same chord were put in a different order, for example A-C-E-G, then it would be more appropriate to give it the symbol Am^7 (A minor seventh chord). In this case, C^6 and Am^7 are synonymous for one and the same chord. This chord has two names.

This concept of chord interpretation is often applied in (jazz) improvisation. Some of the basic chord synonyms, which can be transposed into all keys, are contained in the following list:

Chord Synonyms in C Major		
Chord Symbol	**Chord Notes**	**Possible Synonyms**
C^{sus4}	C-F-G	F^{sus2}
C^6	C-E-G-A	Am^7
$C^{6/9}$ (o. 1)	E-G-A-D	$A^{7/sus4}$
$C^{6/9 \, sus4}$	C-F-A-D	$F^{6/9}$
$C^{13/sus4}$	C-F-G-A	F^{add9}
Cm^6	C-E♭-G-A	$Am^{7/♭5}$
Cm^7	C-E♭-G-B	$E♭^{\,6}$
$Cm^{6/9}$	C-E♭-G-A-D	$Am^{7/11/♭5}$
$C^{7/♭9}$ (o. 1)	(C)-E-G-B♭-D♭	$D♭^o$, E^o, G^o, $B♭^o$
$C^{7/♯9/♯11}$ (♭5)	C-E-B♭-D♯-G♭	$G♭^{\,7/6/♯11}$

73

List of Chords

In order to gain an idea of the vast number of chords, the following pages provide a list of the most important chords with the tonic of C. They are shown with their names and listed according to "chord families": major, minor and dominant seventh, as well as diminished and augmented chords. First of all the root position of each chord is listed, followed by three possible voicings.

Major Chords

Minor Chords

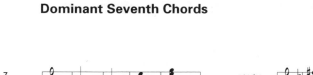

Dominant Seventh Chords

C^7

$C^{7/sus4}$

$C^{7/9}$

$C^{7/9/13}$

$C^{7/9/\#11\,(\flat5)}$

$C^{7/9/\flat13\,(5)}$

$C^{7/\flat9}$

$C^{7/\flat9/\#11\,(\flat5)}$

$C^{7/\flat9/13}$

$C^{7/\#9}$

$C^{7/\#9/\#11\,(\flat5)}$

$C^{7/\#11\,(\flat5)}$

$C^{7/13}$

$C^{7/\flat13\,(\#5)}$

Diminished and Augmented Chords

C^{o7}

C^{+}

6. Musical Instruments

Instrumental Groups

Depending on the type of sound produced, instruments are divided into various groups. The most important of these are:

1. Chordophones (String instruments)

The sound-producing agent is a stretched string. Examples of chordophones (Gr. *Corda* = string) include string and plucked instruments, as well as the piano and harpsichord.

2. Aerophones (Wind Instruments)

In the case of these instruments, the sound-generating medium is an enclosed column of air. Included in this group of instruments are woodwind and brass instruments, the organ and harmonium (e.g. mouth organ and accordion). The name aerophone is taken from the Greek word *aero* = air.

3. Membranophones

For the membranophone (from Gr. *membrana* = skin) instruments, stretched skin is the sound-producing agent. Together with the idiophone instruments, the membranophones are often listed as part of the **percussion group**. This group is subdivided into those instruments that produce a sound of **definite pitch** (kettledrum, glockenspiel, xylophone, etc.) and those that **do not** (snare drum, cymbals, triangle, etc).

4. Idiophones

All instruments, which consist simply of elastic material (metal, wood) capable of producing sound belong to this group. Examples are xylophone, bells, triangle, vibraphone, gong. This group of instruments takes its name from the Greek word *idios* = self

5. Electrophones

This group of instruments includes both traditional instruments with electrical amplification (E-guitar and E-bass) as well as all instruments with electronically produced sound (synthesizer, E-organ, keyboards, etc.).

The borders between these groups are not firmly fixed, some instruments can be placed in more than one category. For instance, the piano (forte) is often put in the percussion group, because its sound is produced by hammers.

There are also other criteria for classification purposes. A group of instruments with keys can be formed to include the piano, grand piano (string instruments) as well as organ (sound produced by an enclosed column of air) and synthesizer.

The following pages show the most important instruments with details on tuning, the clefs used for their notation and their approximate range. Depending on how the instrument is made and the ability of the performing musician, these can vary considerably.

Transposing Instruments

In the case of some instruments (belonging, for example, to the clarinet and saxophone families, the bassoons, trumpets and horns), the written music and the actual sound are not identical. The instrumental voice is transposed (L; *transponere* = translate), that is why these instruments are called **transposing instruments**.

In the following summaries, both the basic key of the instrument (e.g. E♭ clarinet or basset horn in F) as well as its actual sound are listed. The addition of *in F* or *A clarinet* is always in relation to the tone of C and indicates the transposition: C is written, but either F or A sounds. Nowadays the music for transposing instruments is often written as it sounds, which makes the work of the composer much easier, but demands a constant reorientation from the musician while playing.

Chordophones

Classical String Instruments

In classical music the string instruments are really the most important group of instruments consisting of violin, viola, violincello (in short: cello) and double-bass. Originally the double-bass was not a member of the violin family, it came much later.

In a classical orchestra, the strings play in the following combination: first violin, second violin, viola, cello, double-bass.

In chamber music, the first violin, second violin, viola and cello form an ensemble, called a string quartet.

Violin, soprano range

Tuning of the open strings

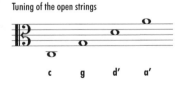

g   d'   a'   e''

Range

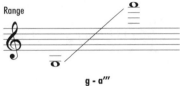

g - a'''

Viola, Alto range

Tuning of the open strings

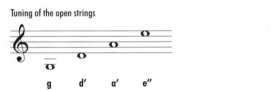

c   g   d'   a'

Range

c - a'''

Cello, alto range

Tuning of the open strings

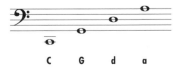

C   G   d   a

Range

c - b''

Double-bass, bass range

Tuning of the open strings

E_1 A_1 D   G

Range

$E_1 - a'$

There is also a five-stringed version of the double-bass, tuned to C_1 - E_1 - D – G, as well as one in solo tuning: $F\sharp_1$ - B_1 - E – A.

The range of all string instruments can be extended upwards quite considerably by playing so-called "harmonics".

Plucked Instruments

Guitar

The guitar is a transposing instrument, it sounds an octave lower than written. There are a large number of special forms of the guitar, which vary very considerably in regard to construction, number of strings and method of playing (E-guitar, 12-stringed guitar, guitars with several necks etc.). The range and notation of these special forms often differ from the traditional classical (or Spanish) guitar.

Classical Guitar

Tuning: E A d g b e'
Notation and range: E - b'''
Clef used: G-clef

Notation

Sounding Pitch

Tablature for Guitar

Besides the traditional notation, there is another widely-used notation system for the guitar, the **tablature**. Tablature notation is a system which is much older than notation. In the tablature system, the horizontal lines represent the strings. The numbers indicate the fret which is to be played on.

Quite often there are additional markings, which indicate the exact length of the individual notes.

Another important form of notation for the guitar are the **chord diagrams**. They are used to show how a certain chord is played. In chord diagrams, the horizontal lines represent the strings, the verticals are the frets, i.e the space between them.

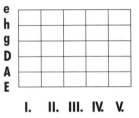

The fingers of the playing hand are numbered:

1 = Index finger   **3** = Ring finger
2 = Middle finger   **4** = Little finger

Open strings played in a chord are marked with a small circle at the side of the diagram; strings which should not be played with an „x". The diagrams indicate the exact position of the chord on the fret board.

This diagram is read as follows:

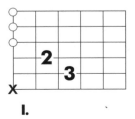

The low E string is not played.

The third finger frets the A string on the 3rd fret, the second finger frets the D string on the 2nd fret.

G, B, and high E are played as "open" (non-fretted) strings.

Rhythmic Notation

A special form of notation called **rhythmic or rhythm notation** is used, particularly when writing for the guitar. In this system, only the rhythm is notated, very often with the addition of a chord symbol:

This form of notation is mostly used to avoid overburdening the music with a lot of chords written out in full, it can therefore also be counted as one of the **abbreviations**.

Bass Guitar

The bass guitar is a transposing instrument, it sounds an octave lower than the written notes. Five- and six-stringed instruments in various tunings are also used.

83

Harp (Pedal Harp)

On the harp, there is a string for each natural note.
Using the pedal, the natural notes can be tuned a half-step higher or lower. In this way, the harp can be played in every key.

Range

C♭ - g♭''''

Other Plucked Instruments

This list also includes some other chordophone instruments with details on tuning, notation and range. In the main, they are used in folk music, and occasionally in classical music to add a special color.

Mandolin

Tuning: g d' a' e''
Notation and range: g-a'''
Clef used: G-clef

Lute

Tuning: varies according to historical background and region
Notation and range: e-f♯'''; Range: E- f♯''
Clef used: G-clef

Zither

Tuning: varies according to historical background and region
Notation and range: F1-d''''
Clef used: F-clef and G-clef

The mandolin, lute and zither are members of large families, where the number of strings, tuning, notation and playing techniques vary due to historical and regional factors.

Grand Piano, Piano (forte)

The piano (forte) has a different construction to that of the grand piano: while the strings of the grand piano are in a horizontal position, the piano's strings are vertical. Both instruments are built in various sizes, which considerably influence the fullness of the tone. There is no difference in the way the tone is produced: the strings are struck by hammers which are activated by the keys. Both instruments are played in the same way. The standard keyboard usually has 88 (black and white) keys.

Most piano music is written on two staves joined together by a **brace**.
The music for the left hand is written on the F clef, and on the G-clef for the right hand. Occasionally some piano music requires more than two clefs.

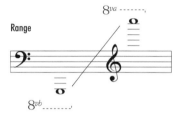

Harpsichord

Even though the harpsichord is a stringed keyboard instrument like the grand piano, there are however decisive differences.
Here the sound is produced through a mechanism which strikes the strings in the manner of a plucked instrument and, on releasing the key, is immediately mute.

Aerophones (Wind Instruments)

Recorder

Even though the recorder (in its descant form) is probably the best-known woodwind instrument resulting from present-day musical education, it is not a member of the symphony orchestra. In the early 20th century it was re-discovered for teaching music, as this inexpensive instruments is easy to learn to play.

It is, however, firmly anchored in "Early Music" (before the 18th century). The recorder is made in five sizes: sopranino, descant, treble, tenor and bass. Contrary to most other woodwind instruments, the recorder does not have any keys, which close the holes. The whistle mouthpiece is a wide-tapered conical bore.

Flute

Although the cylindrical pipe is made of metal (mostly silver), the flute belongs to the woodwind group of instruments, as metal was first used for the main body in the 19th century. The flute is a non-transposing instrument in C, the notation and sound are identical and its music is written on the G-clef.

Related instruments are the alto flute (transposing and built in G, F, and E♭) and the piccolo, which has the highest register in the orchestra.

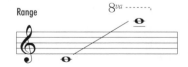

Range

Oboe

For this instrument, the sound is produced by two reeds (a double reed), separated by a slight opening, which vibrate against each other in the mouth cavity. It consists of a conical pipe (top joint and lower joint), and in some related forms a bell.
Music for the oboe is written on the G-clef, it does not transpose. One particular form of the oboe is the oboe d'amore (a transposing instrument in A).

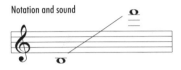

Notation and sound

Cor Anglais

The English horn, often referred to by its French name „cor anglais", belongs to the oboe family and is also known as the alto oboe. It is easily recognisable by its curved mouthpiece.
Music is written on the G-clef; it is a transposing instrument, sounding a fifth lower than written.

Notation   Sound

Bassoon

The bassoon is the bass of the woodwind instruments in the orchestra. It consists of two parallel tubes connected by a horizontal U-shaped bar.

The sound is produced the same way as for the oboe - through a double reed.

The bassoon is not a transposing instrument. Depending on the range of the music, it is written either solely on the F-clef or on both the F- and G-clefs.

Range

Double Bassoon or Contra Bassoon

The double bassoon, the bass of the bassoon family, consists of four tubes connected to each other. The double bassoon is a transposing instrument. Music is written in the F-clef and sounds an octave lower than written.

Notation

Sound

Clarinet

The clarinet is not only an important instrument of the woodwind group in classical music. During the 20th century it became very popular also in the world of jazz.
It would also be difficult to imagine the many branches of dance music and folk music without the clarinet.
The clarinet has a distinct variation of timbre in different ranges, the high tones often harsh and shrill, the lower register being more hollow and soft.
The clarinet has a mouthpiece, known as the "beak", a single reed which produces the sound and a cylindrical pipe made of wood with a bell-shaped opening at the end. The clarinet is in the key of B♭, E♭, A and C (not transposing).

Clarinet in B♭

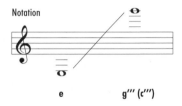

Notation

e   g''' (c''')

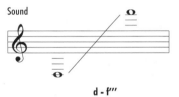

Sound

d - f'''

Clarinet in A

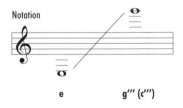

Notation

e   g''' (c''')

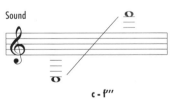

Sound

c - f'''

Clarinet in E♭

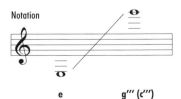

Notation

e   g''' (c''')

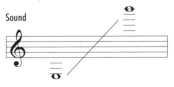

Sound

g - b'''

Saxophone

The saxophone was invented around 1840 by Adolphe Sax. It is rarely played in a classical orchestra. However the saxophone has a prominent place in jazz bands and pop music of the 20th century.
The body of the instrument is of metal (brass). Despite this, the saxophone counts as a member of the woodwind family as (as in the case of the clarinet) the sound is produced through a single beating reed, which is fixed to a beak-shaped mouthpiece. The saxophone belongs to the clarinet group of instruments.

The complete family of saxophones numbers seven: sopranino, soprano, alto, tenor, baritone, contrabass, and subcontrabass. The sopranino and soprano have a straight body, the others the characteristic curved form.
Those used most frequently are:

Soprano Saxophone in B♭

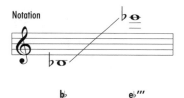

Alto Saxophone in E♭

Tenor Saxophone in B♭

Notation

b♭   f'''

Sound

A♭   e♭''

Baritone Saxophone in E♭

Notation

b♭   f'''

Sound

D♭   a♭'

Horn (actually: French Horn)

The French horn is a brass instrument with a funnel-shaped mouthpiece and a narrow conical bore wound into a spiral and ending in a large flaring bell with three valves. The sounds are produced through the tension of the vibrating lips.
In the orchestra, the horns usually play as a four-part group. The horn is held in an unusual way: the bell faces back and not in the direction of the listener.

The horn is normally in the key of F, and sometimes in B♭. All horns are transposing instruments. Occasionally there is a requirement for a horn in E♭ (mostly in military bands).

Related forms are the hunting horn, and the parforce horn, a special type of hunting horn.

French Horn in F

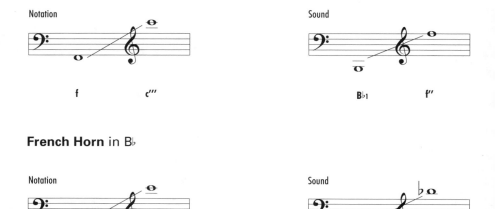

Notation

f   c'''

Sound

B♭1   f''

French Horn in B♭

Notation

Sound

Trombone

The trombone is a brass instrument, where the tone is changed by a U-shaped middle piece being moved to and from the player by means of a crossbar and is called a slide. This enables a glissando movement from note to note. For the valve trombone, the slide is replaced by valves.

An orchestra usually has a group of three trombones. Music is written on the F-clef, occasionally also on the C-clef (tenor clef). It sounds as notated.

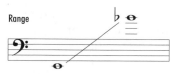

Range

Tuba

It was only in the 19th century that the tuba was introduced into the orchestra. It gained greater popularity in jazz bands, especially at the beginning of the 20th century. Special forms of tuba, which the player hangs over the shoulders, were designed for marching bands (helicon, sousaphone).
Although the tuba belongs to the transposing instruments, it sounds as notated. There are tubas in the key of C, F, E♭ and B♭.

Tuba in F

Range

Tuba in E♭

Range

Tuba in B♭

Range

Trumpet

The trumpet takes the same position in the brass instruments as the violin amongst the strings. The trumpet has the highest register of all brass instruments. In jazz, it is one of the most important (solo) instruments.

There is a trumpet in the key of C which is non-transposing and also one in B♭ (transposing). The trumpet in B♭ is more commonly used. Special varieties are the trumpet in E♭, which is only used in brass bands and the bass trumpet in B♭ (range: B♭1-d''). The cornet also belongs to the trumpet family.

Trumpet in B♭

Notation

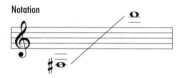

Sound

Percussion Instruments

Timpani

The percussionist of an orchestra uses a large number of percussion instruments. They can be divided into two groups, those that produce a sound of definite pitch and those that do not. The large and small kettle drums are the most important percussion instruments:

The two drums can be tuned as required (depending on the type, also while being played). Often there is a requirement for a group of four drums.

Percussion Instruments

As there is an almost indeterminable variety of percussion instruments (whether membranophones or idophones), it is impossible to mention them all. For this reason, the following list contains only a selection of the best-known and most important percussion instruments.

Snare Drum (Side Drum)

The small drum is a basic component of a set of drums. It is used today under the name of snare drum, as it has a group of gut, silk or steel strings stretched taut across the lower head, which lend it the characteristic sound.

Tom Tom

Tom Toms are either fixed on a stand or hung on the shoulder and used mostly in dance bands. They are made in various sizes and models.

Bass Drum

This large drum varies considerably in size and model. In the orchestra it is usually on a stand. In a drum set, the bass drum usually stands on the floor and is played with a pedal. In marching bands, the drum is usually carried.

Cymbals

Cymbals are large circular brass plates in various sizes. The sound is produced by clashing them together (as Hi-Hat in a drum set) or by striking a single cymbal with a drum stick. These are just two of a number of sound-producing methods.

Xylophone

The xylophone consists of a row of wooden bars, that are arranged like a keyboard and struck with a stick. It has a range of about three octaves. It is closely related to the marimbaphone.

Vibraphone

It is similar in construction to the xylophone, but has metal bars and electrically driven rotating propellers under each one causing a vibrato sound. The bars can be dampened.
There are also many more types of glockenspiels with metal bars.

Chimes

The bells are usually a set of metal tubes, suspended in a frame, and played vertically.

Gong, Tamtam

There is often confusion over these two instruments, as the name gong is used mostly for all instruments of this sort. A gong is a bronze circular disk of definite pitch, whereas the tamtam has no definite pitch. Very often the middle of the gong is slightly convex.

Other Percussion Instruments

The number of (Latin-American) percussion instruments is indeterminable for amateurs. They come from South American folk music and are now firmly established in European music.

Claves are two wooden sticks, that are struck together.

Guiro is a wooden tube with notches, which is scraped with a stick.

Maracas are wooden shell shakers filled with dry seeds or little stones.

Chocallo is a wooden tube, filled with little stones

The **cowbell** is a small bell, that is held in the hand and struck with a drumstick.

Agogo consists of two bells, each of a different pitch, firmly tied to each other.

Cabasa was originally a pumpkin entwined with necklaces; today mostly a cylinder with metal chains is used.

Percussion Notation

There is no uniform notation system for percussion.
The principle of the various systems is identical: each line of the stave is allotted to one percussion instrument. As many percussion instruments are often used, extra symbols are added to the established note heads in order to fit everything on the five lines of the stave, These special symbols also indicate the desired technique to be used:

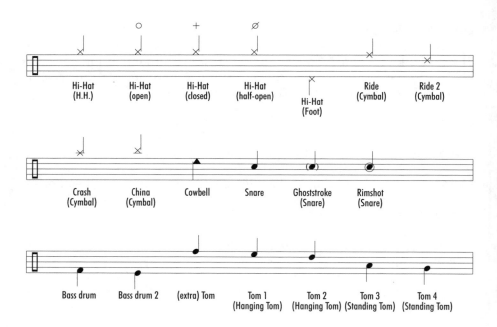

Stems of notes pointing upwards indicate playing with sticks, while those pointing downwards indicate the use of the pedal (with feet).

Electrophones

It is almost impossible to subdivide the electrophone instruments, as there are vast individual differences in regard to type, mechanism, playing technique and sound.

In principle, instruments with purely electronically produced oscillations (E-organ, keyboard, synthesizer) can be separated from those produced their sound mechanically (E-guitar, E-bass).

But even here the differences are only between individual and not groups of instruments. For instance, the E-organs, which originally produced oscillations by mechanical-electrical means (Hammond organ with rotating metal disks) are now almost all electronic instruments.

Organ

The organ is the forerunner of the electronic keyboard instruments (synthesizer, sampler and E-organ). Even though it was originally only used in church music, it's now found in every large concert hall. It is one of the most extensive and complicated instruments used in music. The description as "Queen of the Instruments" conveys some idea as to what effect the diversity of organ sounds had on listeners in past centuries.

The sound is produced through pipes, which (depending on the tone color) offer a huge variety. A group of pipes of the same tone color is known as a register. The organ is played on a keyboard, a fact which makes it difficult to agree in which group of instruments it should be placed.

Voices/Registers

The names of the four main human registers referred originally only to voices, but later however also to instruments of corresponding registers.
These names are of Latin origin:

- **Soprano** (L. *supremus* = highest) or **Treble** describes the high female voice or child's voice,
- **Contralto** (L. *altus* = high) the low female voice. The misleading name comes from the historical development in 13th and 14th century, when this register was still that of a high male voice.
- **Tenor** (L. *tenere* = to hold) the high male voice, and
- **Bass** (L. *bassus* = low) the low male voice.

The two middle registers **Mezzo-soprano** (It. *mezzo* = middle) and **Baritone** (It. *baritono* = low sounding, sonorous) were added later to the traditional four main voices.

Range of Voices

The exact range of each voice depends on the natural talent, as well as training and fitness of the singer and can therefore not always be determined. The range of the individual voices are roughly:

Female voices
- **Soprano**   (a) c' - a'' (c''', in individual cases also up to f''')
- **Mezzo-soprano**   g - f''
- **Contralto**   (f) a - f'' (b'')

Male voices
- **Tenor**   (B-flat) c - a' (c'')
- **Baritone**   A - g'
- **Bass**   (D) E - e' (f')

The notes in brackets indicate the range required of a soloist. Individual well-trained singers can however, often go well beyond these given ranges.

In Early music, the music for voices was written on the C-clef, but in more modern music only the G-clef and the F-clef are used. The charts show the range of the clefs which are used:

Female Voices

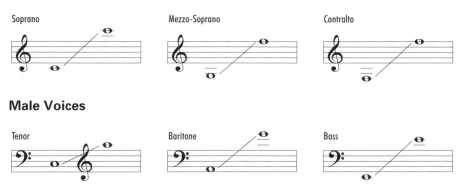

Male Voices

As the individual ranges overlap each other, it is sometimes difficult in practice to differentiate for example between a low soprano and a high contralto.

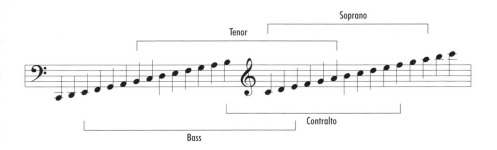

In the case of opera singers, the voices are classified according to type, timbre and other characteristics, e.g. dramatic soprano, coloratura soprano, lyrical contralto, etc.
These classifications provide the experts with information on the suitability of a voice for a certain role in an opera.

Appendix

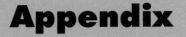

Clefs

The clefs used today are divided into families according to the name of the note they pinpoint. The most important of these are the **G-clef**, the **C-clef** and the **F-clef**.

G-Clef

The most important **G-clef** is the **violin clef**. There is also occasional use of a modified form, with a super- or subscript 8, indicating the transposition of an octave up or down.

C-Clef

The **C-clefs**, are another branch of the clef family. This clef was used in the 16th century for a-cappella singing, whereby each voice part was given its own clef and it was named after that voice. Music publishers today have put most music written in the C-clef for instruments or voice in the violin or bass clefs .

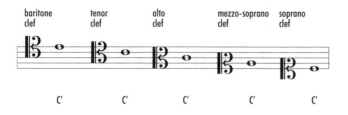

F-Clef

The most important **F-clef** is the **bass clef**. There is also occasional use of a modified form, with a subscript 8, indicating transposition of an octave down.

Percussion Clef

The so-called percussion clef is a special case. It is used for the notation of instruments with no definite pitch.

The most important values of note and rests

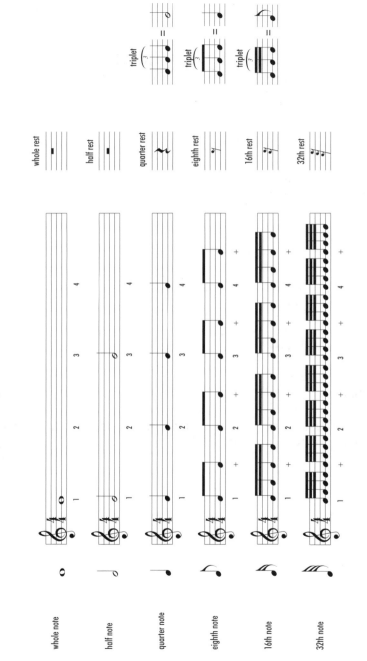

Pitch Equivalents

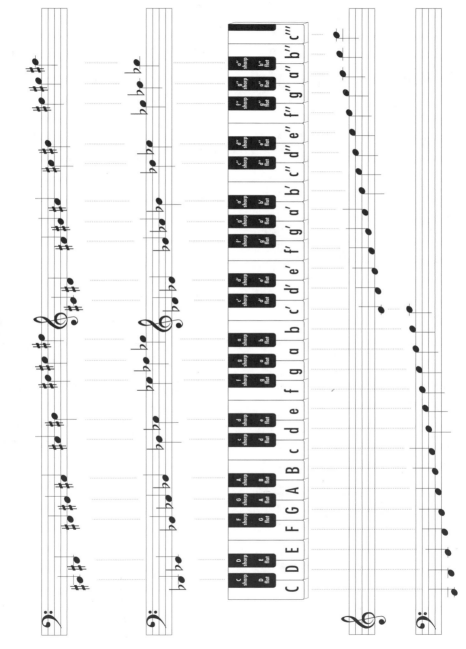

The most important time signatures

The following are the most important time signatures (also referred to as metric signatures) showing how the accents are placed. Main accents are highlighted in dark grey, subsidiary accents in light grey:

Major Scales

Minor Scales

Italian Tempo Marks

At the beginning of a piece of music there is very often an Italian mark for the tempo. Contrary to the precise markings such as ♩ = 120 or 120 bpm, this information indicates approximately the desired tempo, leaving the musician a certain amount of freedom in determining the exact tempo.

The following list is by no means complete, but contains the most frequently used tempo marks:

prestissimo	extremely fast	
vivacissimo	extremely fast	
presto	(very) fast	168-208 bpm
vivace	lively	
allegro	fast, playful	120-168 bpm
allegretto	not so fast, merrily	
moderato	moderately	108-120 bpm
andantino	moving moderately	
andante	walking pace	76-108 bpm
grave	grave solemn	
adagio	slowly	66-76 bpm
lento	slowly	
larghetto	fairly slow	60-66 bpm
largo	slow, broad	40-60 bpm
larghissimo	very broad	

Italian Expression Marks

Just as there are Italian tempo marks, there are also "expression marks". These are indications by the composer on the general tone or mood of the piece.

As these terms cannot be given measured value, the musician is left to interpret, as in the case of tempo.

Amabile	amiably
Appassionato	passionately
Arioso, cantabile	singing
Brillante	brilliantly
Buffo	with humor
capriccioso	moodily
dolce	softly
con dolore	with anguish
espressivo	with expression
furioso	tempestuous
giocoso	jokingly
grazioso	gracefully
maestoso	majestically
scherzando	playful

Italian Dynamic Marks

The field of dynamics can be divided into two parts:

1. Graduated Dynamics

These dynamics deal with volume and thrive on the contrasting loud (forte) and soft (piano). Within this scala of intensity, there are a great number of nuances. The most important are listed here:

fff	*fortissimo possible*	
	fortefortissimo	as loud as possible
ff	*fortissimo*	very loud
f	*forte*	loud
mf	*mezzoforte*	half loud
mp	*mezzopiano*	half soft
p	*piano*	soft
pp	*pianissimo*	very soft
ppp	*pianissimo possible*	
	pianopianissimo	as soft as possible

Further additions and variations which are frequently used:

meno f	meno forte	less loud
più p	più piano	softer
meno p	meno piano	less softly
più f	più forte	louder (più=more)
fp,sfp	fortepiano	loud and immediately soft again
sf, sfz, fz	sforzato	sudden strong accent

2. Gradual Dynamics

These terms describe a slow, gradual increase or decrease in volume.

Here the most important expressions are:

becoming louder/stronger: *Crescendo (cresc.),*
Rinforzando (rfz.),
Sempre più f

Becoming softer/weaker: *decrescendo (decresc.),*
diminuendo (dim.),
sempre meno f

The signs for *cresc./decresc.*, the so-called „crescendo fork", are indicated as follows:

Cresc.	or	$<$	= to become louder
Decresc.	or	$>$	= to become softer

Basic Guitar Chords

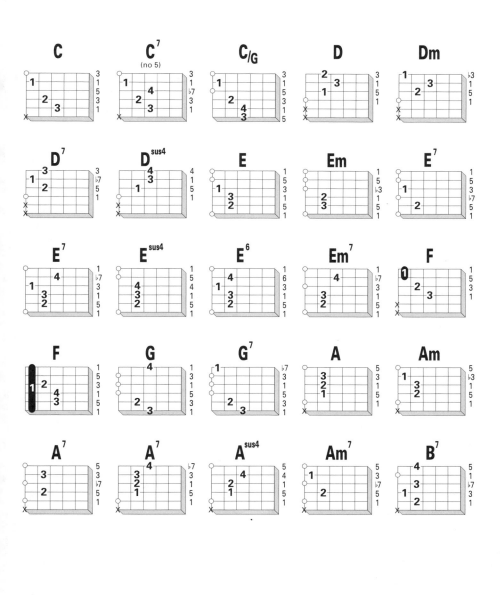

Index

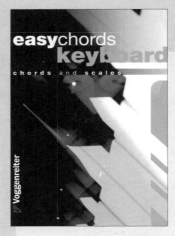